BUSINESS PLAN CHECKLIST

Plan your way to business success

Written by Antoine Delers
In collaboration with Brigitte Feys
Translated by Carly Probert

Business 50MINUTES.com

BUSINESS PLAN CHECKLIST

KEY INFORMATION

- **Names:** Business plan, development plan
- **Uses:** Generally used to create new businesses or launch new products, a business plan allows the feasibility of a project to be assessed, taking into account the characteristics of the market, and defines the marketing plan.
- **Why is it successful?** A business plan helps to identify the limits and the prospects of a business project by detailing all of the points relating to the launch of the business: product, market, resources, etc. It is compulsory when a new company is being set up and when external financing is being received, and helps to establish the short- and medium-term strategy and financial profitability of the project, as well as the key success factors. The forecasts and strategies set out in the business plan are then used to monitor the smooth running of the company's activities and, if necessary, to make adjustments in order to achieve the objectives that were initially set as efficiently as possible.
- **Key words:**
  - <u>Financial plan:</u> a plan detailing the financial inputs and outputs of a structure, including in particular the historical and projected assessments and income statements.
  - <u>Market:</u> strictly speaking, all of the companies, customers, suppliers and other intermediaries involved in the same activity; more broadly, it includes the products, raw materials and third parties that interact

with the market.
- ◦ <u>Market research:</u> qualitative and/or quantitative analysis of different stakeholders, such as customers, suppliers, competitors and market trends.
- ◦ <u>Marketing mix:</u> the coherent combination of the price, product, place and promotion variables of an activity (communication), directed towards the consumer to encourage them to buy.
- ◦ <u>PESTLE analysis:</u> the study of the macroeconomic factors (political, economic, socio-cultural, technological, environmental and legal) of the environment which may influence the development of a business. This analysis does not address the microeconomic environmental factors, which, although also outside the company, are specific to a business's sector of activity.
- ◦ <u>SWOT analysis:</u> the study of the internal and external environment which allows the strengths, weaknesses, opportunities and threats related to a specific company to be identified.

INTRODUCTION

The origin of the business plan coincides with a growing desire to establish and ensure a degree of stability, particularly in terms of funding, for a new venture (realisation of a project, creation of a business, etc.). To describe the future situation of a business project, with the aim of making this happen, a business plan is needed. It was particularly during the 1970s – a period which saw a proliferation of crises and cross-sectorial changes (due to oil crises and the arrival of computers) – that this tool became essential to start and run a company effectively. It allows users to attract the attention of decision-makers, managers, bankers, etc. These are all potential stakeholders who, if they see the potential for profit, may wish to invest in the project.

Definition of the model

The business plan provides information to managers, shareholders and potential lenders by delivering an overview of the (new) company, its development models, its strategic choices and its environment. In concrete terms, the document mainly describes:

- **The company and its main features**, through a description of its strategy and future goals, a study of the strengths and weaknesses of the (new) company and, finally, a presentation of the future team;
- **The market and customers,** through market research that informs the third parties of the state of the market (its growth, its potential, etc.), customers (purchasing behaviour, etc.), competitors, suppliers and other key intermediaries.
- **The expected competition**, which lists the main strengths of the competitors, including the competitive advantages that the (new) company will try to gain;
- **The marketing plan**, which details the proposed marketing strategy for the product or service;
- **The operational plan**, which describes the organisation of the company on a daily basis, particularly through an analysis of the value chain and the different procedures;
- **The financial plan**, which completes the business plan by projecting the financial forecast over several years,

including the expected return on investment (ROI). This is the section that will interest the investors and bankers most. It mainly includes the expected revenues and expenses during the first few years of launch, but also the investment plan, the various financial partners targeted and the projected balance sheets and income statements.

THEORY

Although the term has existed for over a century, the use of the business plan did not spread until the late 1960s and early 1970s (the end of the 'cultural decade' of the Sixties and the emergence of the oil crises starting in 1973). At that time, two major changes were observed:

- the reluctance of investors;
- the emergence and development of IT.

THE RELUCTANCE OF INVESTORS

Following the crises that discouraged investors, it became necessary for businesses in search of financing to design and pay attention to their project presentation in order to effectively convince potential shareholders. Their pitch had to be structured, professional and as realistic as possible.

The inversion of the supply and demand curve encouraged investors to be more cautious in their financing: they now wanted to ensure that they did not overlook any details. With the drop in demand coinciding with a proliferation of increasingly risky projects, it became essential to be able to ensure, thanks to a stable foundation – i.e. an objective and realistic business plan – that the company was definitely viable. Also linked to this change, the increased competitivity required entrepreneurs to be more rigorous in their work (choice and anticipation of potential risks) when creating a business or launching a new product, leading them to conduct a preliminary study to confirm the prospects of success.

THE EMERGENCE AND DEVELOPMENT OF IT

The second change is linked to the appearance of computers in households and intangible (virtual) products. The rise of Silicon Valley in the United States, the birthplace of technology companies, contributed to this development. On the one hand, the creation of many startups required significant investment. On the other hand, investors needed to ensure the viability and ROI of the projects they financed.

THE SITUATION TODAY

Nowadays, drawing up a business plan has become virtually indispensable for the management and creation of new activities, or even for the abandonment of certain activities and the consequent redeployment of resources. Leaders need a solid and consistent base to work from, and investors require certain pieces of vital information to invest their money with confidence. In a small number of cases, the absence of this document is justified. These cases will be discussed in the section on the limitations of the model.

THE 9 KEY STEPS TO SUCCESS – THE CLASSIC BUSINESS PLAN

The business plan is a future forecast for a project, its strategy and its financial statements. Although there is no one correct way to create it (variants are possible, and a business plan can include between seven and 12 chapters), we have chosen to present the plan in nine sections.

1. Executive summary
2. Presentation of the company and the management team
3. Market research
4. Analysis of the customer base
5. Analysis of the competition
6. Marketing plan
7. Operational plan
8. Financial plan
9. Appendices

Executive summary

The executive summary (or management summary) is a one- or two-page overview of the project, intended for the relevant executives and third parties. This summary should succinctly present the main guiding principles of the business plan: the type of products and services created, the strategy implemented, the customers, and finally the financial data, including the ROI. It must be complete to allow the reader to quickly get an idea of the potential of the project.

Presentation of the company and the management team

The second part of the business plan concerns the company itself, its overall strategy, its short-, medium- and long-term objectives, as well as its strengths and aspirations (future challenges). At this stage of the study, it may be worth using a SWOT analysis to describe the company and its environment: the entrepreneur can take this opportunity to identify the strengths, weaknesses, opportunities and threats.

SWOT analysis

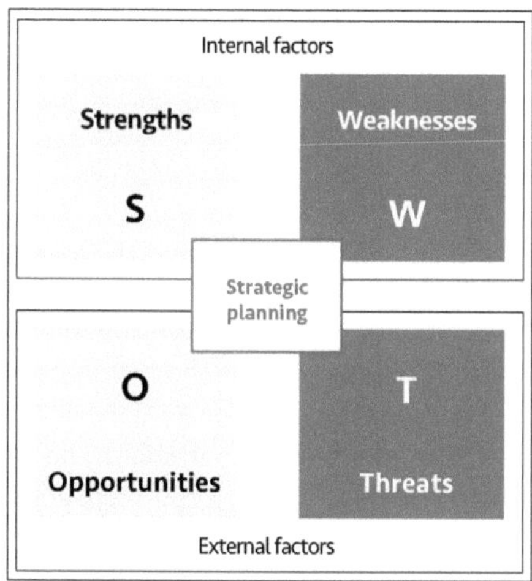

In a SWOT analysis, the strengths are the inherent assets of the company, such as its location in a place conducive to business, while the weaknesses represent the (internal) disadvantages. Finally, opportunities and threats (external factors) identify the future prospects of the company. It is up to the company to take advantage of the opportunities while avoiding threats and to correct weaknesses using its strengths.

The short-, medium- and long-term objectives of the company must also be defined here: growth in market share, increase in the number of customers, increased profitability, etc.

Finally, the presentation of the company includes a description of the management team, meaning the experience, contributions and future responsibilities of the partners who will launch and manage the company.

Market research

Market research presents the market as a whole, along with factors outside the business that could have some influence over the future company (or the future of the company). The aim of this section is not to describe the customers and their behaviour, but to present more broadly the composition of the current market, the trends that should be expected, the legislation in place, etc. To get a complete and accurate overview of the external situation, a PESTLE analysis can be carried out. This presents the macroeconomic environment through a framework of six factors.

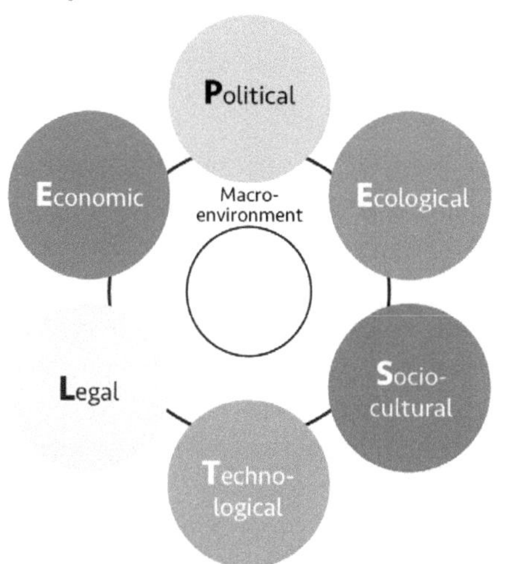

- **Political.** How much governmental pressure is there? How politically stable is the situation?
- **Economic.** What are the interest rates and growth rates? What is the monetary policy?
- **Socio-cultural.** What is the demographic situation? What social legislation is in place?
- **Technological.** What technologies and new patents are available?
- **Ecological.** What are the environmental standards? What sustainable development policy is in place?
- **Legislative.** What are the laws in force in the sector? What consumer protection exists?

This type of analysis seeks to confirm the suitability and legitimacy of setting up a new company on the market.

Market research

Market research is usually the foundation of any business plan. It is an almost compulsory step, as it allows the entrepreneur to become aware of the real conditions of the market that their company is or will be a part of. However, it is often neglected because it takes time, and the people working on the project would rather spend this time on tangible actions to set up the company. Market research is used when seeking to:

- Identify market trends, to see if the target market is favourable or not to the new company.
- Define the target customers, their origins and their buying behaviour.
- Get to know the competition better. Are the competitors well-established? What products do they offer? What are their strengths or competitive advantages?
- Find out about the aspects related to suppliers (their numbers, agreements and possible margins).
- Identify other influences, such as the location, trade laws, social norms and other partners.

Analysis of the customer base: who are the target customers?

The analysis of the customer base is one of the most important points to be developed in the business plan, because without customers, there will obviously not be much money coming in! The analysis therefore aims to describe the customer base to be targeted in the future. At this stage, we must clearly see who makes it up, how to segment it, which catchment area to choose, etc. Statistical institutes can usually provide a significant part of this information.

Consumer needs, meaning what consumers want, should also feature prominently in this section in order to define the characteristics of target customers. Market research in the field is therefore necessary in order to observe the buying habits and desires of consumers, their purchasing power and the price they are willing to pay, with the aim of producing products that can meet their needs.

Analysis of the competition

It is then necessary to focus more on factors outside the company which play a direct role in its sector and influence the delicate balance of supply and demand. This section aims to highlight the different competitors already established in the market and to analyse their products, the prices they set and their competitive advantages. The goal is to know how the company can overcome them and what competitive advantage it can develop. Although this is difficult to carry out exhaustively, a SWOT analysis of the competitors will identify their strengths and weaknesses.

Finally, a classification of direct and indirect competitors may also prove interesting, and the company should not neglect any of these.

- **Direct competitors** are those that provide a service identical to that of the company to meet a similar need.
- **Indirect competitors** offer a different service, but meet the same need.

Marketing plan or the marketing mix

Thanks to the customer and competition analyses carried out, it then becomes possible to define the outreach strategy for future consumers and design a marketing plan. Also called the 'marketing mix', this plan describes the main elements of the marketing strategy of a product or service.

- **Product.** What is the product or service offered?
- **Price.** Is the price aligned with that of the competitors? How can a price difference influence customer buying behaviour?
- **Place (distribution channels).** In which sales channels will it be distributed? Online? In store?
- **Promotion (communication and diffusion).** What advertising should be used? What tone should be used? What image and values do we want to convey?

The 4 Ps of the marketing mix

This mix of four variables enables the development of a coherent plan for the implementation of a marketing strategy. The main points of the SWOT analysis carried out previously can be used alongside this plan.

THE 7 PS THEORY

Although the 4 Ps are an effective and logical combination for structuring a marketing plan, some people prefer to include another two, three or four elements to add more nuance. This most popular additional variables are 'People', a concept that encompasses the salespeople and their ability to sell, and 'Physical Support', which includes both retail outlets and promotional venues.

Operational plan

This section is dedicated to the management of the company and its daily activities: the organisation of the various departments, interactions with external stakeholders (such as suppliers), etc. It must be able to answer the following questions: How is the company organised internally? How can the product be obtained? What procedures are in place? What related services are outsourced? Finally, depending on the format of the business plan, there are several different ways of presenting the information:

- A chart showing the different departments, possibly with the links between them;
- A detailed month by month plan of the various launch activities, including key milestones in the project;
- An analysis of the value chain, meaning a presentation of activities ranging from the research and development stage to after-sales service.

Financial plan

Since bankruptcies are fairly common nowadays, particularly among startups, the criterion of viability has become crucial: if businesses are not clearly viable, financial backers will be reluctant to invest, thus slowing down the momentum of the economy. Apart from the expected inflows and outflows, the financial plan includes the investment plan, the financial partners targeted and the projected balance sheets and income statements.

This financial plan, which usually covers three years, is certainly one of the most consulted sections of the business plan, because it involves the responsibility of funding providers during the first three years of launch and is of particular interest to bankers and investors, who want to ensure that the company is viable. Investors will focus on the risk in relation to the output and return on investment, while bankers will check that the company will be able to repay loans in the early years. It is worth noting that, although a financial plan can cover five or ten years, projecting too far into the future can lead to inaccurate predictions and even, in some cases, completely false forecasts.

As with the operational plan, this may be outlined in various points as required. It involves:

- **A table of the uses and contributions of financial funds for the launch of the company.** These measures may include startup expenses, tangible and financial assets, inventories, the starting balance, and the different contributions and loans to be taken out.
- **Balance sheets and projected income statements for the first three years.** Here, there is no need to enclose the complete documents (because these can also be included in the appendices section of the business plan): only the most significant figures must be present.

Appendices

Finally, the appendices section contains all the documents and information that cannot be found in the main body of the business plan. It includes a detailed financial plan, market research, the CVs of the founders, copies of company documents, patents and licenses, and any other documents providing relevant information.

PRACTICAL APPLICATION

ADVICE AND TOP TIPS

Concrete applications in business

Besides the two general situations which we have already outlined (starting a business or launching a major project) and for which it is mandatory or recommended to make use of a business plan, this type of document also proves useful for:

- Monitoring the company as it develops over the years, by serving as a reference document, and ensuring that the project does not move too far away from the initial forecasts. In the case of major strategic changes, the business plan can be adapted (the quicker disparities are observed, the sooner they can be tackled).
- Convincing investors and lenders of the project's profitability and the benefits of investing or approving a loan.
- Meeting certain legal requirements, In particular the presentation of a financial plan for the creation of an SA (anonymous company) or an LLC (limited liability company) to be annexed to the statutes deposited with the notary.
- Increasing credibility in the eyes of potential future intermediaries (suppliers, distributors, etc.).

1. The business plan helps to define the ins and outs of the project and to ensure that all the relevant issues have been studied and no grey areas remain. Forgetting to consider fierce competition or a barrier to market entry will be detrimental.
2. Linked to this first advantage, it sets the strategy and ensures the feasibility of the project.
3. This standardised document can be presented and understood by everyone involved, such as investors and lenders. As such, even if banking law does not require the entrepreneur to provide a business plan when requesting a (bank) loan, it will be difficult to raise funds without having one.
4. Finally, the business plan facilitates planning at strategic, operational and financial levels for the first few years, and allows users to assess whether the objectives are being achieved during the launch.

Recommendations for an effective business plan

- **When creating a business plan, think objectively.** It is essential to estimate the various points correctly and logically and, above all, to realise that granting yourself a disproportionate salary at the end of the first year after the launch of a new project is not necessarily realistic.
- **Ensure, as far as possible, that the project is feasible.** This may seem obvious, but being sufficiently profitable

after three years is important for survival.

- **Compare projections with those of competitors.** This will help you determine whether your analysis is appropriate. If this is not the case, correct it immediately.
- **Have the plan approved by experts in the field.** This may involve a one-stop shop for businesses which can point out certain things that are missing, and thus enable you to review your strategy so that your business plan is more adapted to the realities of the market.
- **Have non-experts read the business plan.** A business plan should be readable and understandable by everyone, whether they are specialists in the field or not.
- **Follow the changes of the company based on the business plan and adjust accordingly.** This is one of the major assets of the tool, as it verifies that the intended strategy has been well implemented. It is therefore important that the business plan remains a basis for development and support for the management of the business, and in particular for new activities, in the first few years after the launch.
- **Finally, do not conceal harmful information, do not hide the real risks and do not alter the financial forecasts.** The founders must take responsibility if the company goes bankrupt!

CASE STUDY: BARRACUBA

Our fictional case study concerns the opening of a new café in the town centre by a former student who has not forgotten his university years and would like to reconnect with the sector. He has noticed that not many student activities are organised in his city, and that the few cafes available for students are not very busy. With the help of an old class-mate, he decides to make the project a reality. After having no success with private investors, they plan on turning to a bank and, to be taken seriously, they decide to present them with their business plan (20-30 pages). It is outlined here.

Executive Summary

BarraCuba is a new bar with a trendy atmosphere, mainly aimed at young people. To make the bar more lively, themed parties and small concerts will be organised regularly. Ideally located in the student quarter, this venue offers a bar service, with prices among the lowest in the city.

Presentation of the bar and the team

BarraCuba's strategy focuses mainly on young people, who it wants to attract both during the daytime and in the evening.

SWOT analysis of the new project

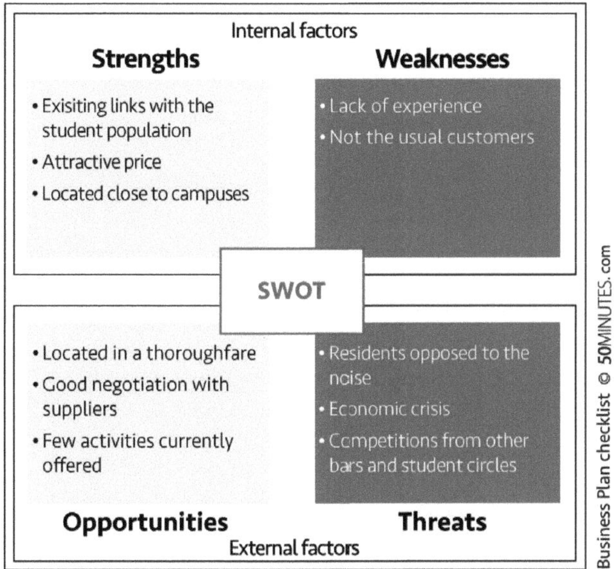

The entrepreneurs also want to create a Spanish coffee shop atmosphere, because they are convinced that the music and dancing will specifically attract a young and trendy crowd.

The company will be represented by Charles. T, a former student and salesman, and Thomas. P, also a former student and accountant. The two partners are each investing $12 500 of their own funds into the business.

Coffee shop market research

This type of analysis, including a PESTLE analysis, among others, focuses on the market of entertainment combined with drinks service. This sector has been experiencing problems for some years, for several reasons.

PESTLE analysis

Political	•Tax increases on alcohol, which affects turnover
Ecological	•Protection of public health linked to alcohol and smoking •Preventative measures against noise nuisance
Socio-cultural	•Proven needs of youths to go out and entertain themselves after work or classes
Technological	•Optic cables in the city, providing a better internet connection
Legal	•Anti-smoking law: smokers can no longer smoke inside a public place
Economic	•Economic crisis which pushes people to pay more attention to their spending and prefer to drink at home •Increase in rent in general, and large fixed costs to bear

However, the market has some strengths and is favourable to the opening of a new bar. Students are always on the lookout for places to relax, meet up and have fun. In addition, the organised events and competitive prices will quickly attract the target audience.

Analysis of the target customers

Their target audience includes university students in the city. Based on a market study focused on the prospects of the project, they find that more than 60% of them are favourable to the opening a bar in the city centre and that 5% of them would be prepared to attend regularly. It should be noted that most of them prefer to go out during the week, as they return home every weekend. The opening of the bar on Friday and Saturday nights would therefore target young workers who do not have the opportunity to go out during the week.

Their secondary customers will be young people aged between 18 and 35. Statistical studies on nightlife in the region show that 20% of young people go out at least once a month, and a further 10% go out every week. The average price spent per night is around $12. Knowing the student sphere well and getting a clear idea of the potential and size of their future customer base, the entrepreneurs assert that they can plan objectively and provide consistent data.

A quantitative estimate of the possible customer base is performed as follows: based on 23% of the 650 000 inhabitants of the city and the surrounding area, they find that young people aged between 18 and 35 total approximately 150 000.

- 20% of them go to a coffee shop or bar once a month (20% of 150 000 x $12)
- 10% go to a coffee shop or bar about four times a month (10% of 150 000 x $12 x 4 visits)

Overall, for the city, the estimated turnover is $1 080 000 per month, or $360 000 + $720 000 (note: this turnover is only an estimate of the market, for all types of outings to bars, and for a full month). If the entrepreneurs add these numbers up over a full year, taking into account the likely drop in consumption during winter and on rainy days (-5% over six months) and the increase in consumption during the nicer seasons (+10% over six months), they manage to achieve an annual turnover of $13 284 000, or $6 156 000 + $7 128 000.

Analysis of the competition

The analysis of the competition was performed on site. The entrepreneurs identified seven other bars within a two-mile radius, which they then analysed. Two of them are student bars: the music is loud there, except during weekday evenings. Both offer an extensive drinks menu, which features a selection of special beers. However, the entrepreneurs, who want to position themselves in this market, think that their lower prices, thanks to a smaller range of drinks, will guarantee them a competitive advantage.

Despite the estimates they have put forward, they say that they are open to changes in strategy depending on the demands, desires and behaviours of their initial customers. Their goal at this stage is to satisfy as many customers as possible, in order to win their loyalty and ensure they speak to others about the bar.

Based on customer and competition data, BarraCuba's market share should rise from 0.5% in the first year to 1.2%

in the second year and 1.5% in the third year.

Forecasts for the first three years

	YEAR 1	YEAR 2	YEAR 3
Market share	0,50 %	1,20 %	1,50 %
Turnover	66 420 €	159 408 €	199 260 €

BarraCuba's marketing plan

In accordance with their vision and market research, they decide to do the following:

BarraCuba's marketing plan

Price	Product	Place	Promotion
• Low and attractive prices, determined according to competitors • Discounts during certain events	• A collection of soft drinks, the majority of traditional beers sold in the sector as well as some special beers • Possible developments	• Situated in the heart of the student quarter, in a thoroughfare	• Posters around campus with practical information on the themed parties • Advertising panels in the window of the bar • ...hopefully a word of mouth effect among students

Operational plan

The daily management of the company will be conducted by the two previously appointed managers:

- Charles T., a salesman, will deal in particular with suppliers, the city council and regulatory bodies, as well as the management of the bar.
- Thomas P., an accountant, will be responsible for the management of funds, accounting/taxation and everything related to financial matters. He will also handle the management of the bar during the evenings.

To start with, they do not plan on subcontracting any activities, apart from any exceptional and unexpected issues relating to legal and technical problems which they cannot deal with themselves. They plan to hire five students, on a part-time basis and with student contracts, to get their business going in order to attract crowds during organised events.

Launch plan for BarraCuba

- Months 1 and 2 – February-March: market research, financial plan and confirmation of the business plan (in progress).
- Months 3 and 4 – April-May: obtaining a bank loan, contacting the owner of the future premises and the city council, and communicating information to citizens.
- Months 5 – June: obtaining licenses and agreements to set up the bar and negotiation of contracts with suppliers.
- Month 6 – July: start of the promotion of the future

venue and search for students to work there.

- Month 7 – August: installation of furniture, concert stage and bar.
- Month 8 – September: official opening of the bar at the start of the new academic year with a special evening and discounts on certain drinks.

Financial plan

Below is the table of the main contributions and uses of funds for the launch.

Financial plan

Use of funding	Origin of funds
•Commercial funds: $ 12,000 •Rental lease (12 months): $ 9,600 •Deposit: $ 1,600 •Fixed assets: $ 2,500 •Layout: $ 600 •Cash register: $ 450 •Advertising: $ 500 •Initial treasury: $ 5,000	•Manager 1 own funds: $ 12,500 •Manager 2 own funds: $ 12,500 •Expected loan: $ 12,250

Looking at their sales estimates, the expected turnover for the first year of launch ('n') is $66 420, the second is $159 408 and the third is $199 260. The expected net profit for the first three years should increase as follows:

- n (launch year): $249 (loss)
- n + 1 (second year): $30,432

- n + 2 (third year): $46, 452

Provisional table of the first launch years

	Year 1	Year 2	Year 3
Turnover	$ 66,420	$ 159,408	$ 199,260
Exploitation charges	$ 20,000	$ 20,000	$ 20,000
Purchase of goods	$ 26,568	$ 63,763.2	$ 79,704
Wage costs	$ 15,000	$ 25,000	$ 25,000
Result of exploitation	$ 4,852	$ 50,644.8	$ 74,556
Taxes and charges	$ 1,601.16	$ 16,712.784	$ 24,603.48
Interest and loans	$ 2,000	$ 2,000	$ 2,000
Other expenses	$ 1,500	$ 1,500	$ 1,500
Net profit	- $ 249.16	$ 30,432.016	$ 46,452.52

The business plan must remain useful beyond the first years after the launch. When the managers of BarraCuba reach the end of the first year (and the following years), they must compare their predictions with what they have achieved, and reflect on the reasons for any discrepancies. Correcting a strategy already in motion is still possible, and the faster this shift takes place, the greater the likelihood of achieving the initial objectives.

LIMITATIONS AND EXTENSIONS

LIMITATIONS AND CRITICISMS

As is the case with any model, there are some criticisms of the business plan.

- **The business plan is only a provisional study of the project, and is therefore not a foolproof guarantee of profitability.** Many unforeseen events may jeopardise the forecasts established: a miscalculation of turnover, a poor estimate of the market, a fall in consumption, an error in product design or a price war with the competition. Nobody can predict the future, but it must be remembered that the business plan will still function as a basis to work from.
- **The regular changes made to the business plan may seem somewhat laborious.** In the case of startups or companies in particularly unsettled sectors (IT, for instance, where products very quickly become obsolete), changes to the plan are common: a change in strategy, improvement of the project, an unexpected change of customers, etc. The initial business plan is no longer relevant, as its outline is too far removed from reality.
- **Lack of resources (time, energy and skills) to draw up a comprehensive and effective business plan.** As it is often long and tedious to produce, the business plan consequently seems unworkable for young entrepreneurs who do not have enough time to devote to it. Market research, product research, the description of the company, and the financial plan will also require

external resources for correction and approval, and they therefore prevent the entrepreneur from focusing on their core business at the beginning. In addition, the fact that they must draw up a business plan may discourage entrepreneurs from pursuing their projects.

- **Few possible alternatives.** Unfortunately, there are few or no alternatives to the business plan. Not having one during fundraising could be detrimental to the new company, as banks and other financial institutions wish to have a solid foundation before investing. However, it is highly likely that this attitude will change one day in favour of simplified business startup studies, as is the case in Canada. However, there are two cases where the business plan is not mandatory: where an entrepreneur decides to supply the necessary funds to start the project themselves; and where companies with a high added value but significant risks rely on individual investors, angel investors or investment funds (however, they will still need to present the few main points of the business plan, namely the future product, its usefulness, the potential customers and the expected turnover).

ANGEL INVESTORS

Angel investors are experienced individual investors (with some equity) who, guided by their intuition, provide funding and offer their protégés their expertise, their business network and their knowledge as partners of the new company. New companies which use this type of investment are often startups with high growth potential, offering innovative solutions in terms of new technology or industrial techniques, or on emerging markets.

RELATED MODELS AND EXTENSIONS

The balanced scorecard

This is a company guiding and management tool based on KPIs (Key Performance Indicators), which provides executives and managers with a clear overview of the important activities underway or due to be implemented. There is no one type of scorecard, because it is adapted to the company. It features generic indicators such as turnover, as well as indicators specific to each sector.

The balanced scorecard can be used in conjunction with the business plan because, by picking up the key figures, it helps to control and monitor the new company throughout its early years. Apart from corporate control, this management tool also allows managers to anticipate problems by establishing provisions in order to tackle them later on, but also to develop a clear strategy. Indeed, thanks to the different strategic areas studied, nothing is left out.

- **Financial axis:** turnover, expected profit, earnings per share (EPS), return on investments (ROI), return on assets (ROA), etc.
- **Customer axis:** market share, level of customer satisfaction, retention rates, etc.
- **Internal processes axis:** duration and cost of produc-

tion, lead time, customer response time, etc.

- **Organisational learning axis:** number of complaints made by employees, internal satisfaction rate, number of training courses attended, development opportunities, etc.

The Gantt chart

This is a project management tool which is regularly used in IT and engineering. It provides a visual representation of the progress of the project, the various milestones (key dates), and what remains to be done. This tool is especially useful for planning company launches.

Gantt chart example

Task	Start	End	June	July	August	Sept.
Comparative study of machines	1/06/15	30/06/15	▬▬▬			
Research suppliers	20/06/15	20/07/15		▬▬▬		
Delivery of machines	20/07/15	10/08/15			▬▬	
Installation of machines	10/08/15	16/08/15			▬	
Initial testing of machines	17/08/15	18/08/15			▪	
Launch of production	18/08/15					▬▬▬

SUMMARY

- The business plan is an operational guide, useful when creating a business or launching a major project, that precisely describes the guidelines and future expectations (for the next three years) while providing a short- and medium-term overview of the project.
- It is designed for executives and project managers, who will need to ensure that the project is feasible and closely monitor its implementation. It will also help to convince investors and inform all collaborators of their tasks and responsibilities.
- The document is divided into around ten chapters and has the following main objectives:
  - Present the product and its benefits through the marketing plan;
  - Describe the environment in and around the company through market research;
  - Provide financial forecasts through the financial plan.
- Its greatest advantage is the fact that it offers a clear outline of the project, with no grey areas. It is essential to be able to determine a clear and effective strategy, both in times of crisis and under normal conditions.
- The business plan is virtually mandatory when applying for funding from public bodies and banks, and does not have many alternatives. Some private investors, such as angel investors, prefer a short and simplified presentation focusing more on the product, its usefulness and the all-important ROI.
- If it is to be effective, a business plan must be drawn up

correctly and objectively. Mistakes should be avoided at all costs and you must not, under any circumstances, conceal damaging information, at the risk of watching your business collapse.

- It is important that people outside the project approve the business plan to ensure that it is reliable and easy to understand.
- Finally, used alongside a balanced scorecard, the business plan should serve as a reference document throughout the early years after the launch of the new company or new project described therein. Entrepreneurs should be able to use it as a benchmark to ensure that the strategy functions as it should and the project is profitable; as necessary, adjustments should be made to targets, changes should be made and new forecasts should be completed.

FURTHER READING

BIBLIOGRAPHY

- Abrams, R. (2014) *The Successful Business Plan: Secrets and Strategies*. Palo Alto: Planning Shop.
- BECI (No date) *Business plan : quels points aborder ?* [Online]. [Accessed 28 April 2015]. Available from: <http://www.beci.be/services/je_cree_ma_societe/business_plan_quels_points_aborder/>
- Entrepreneur (No date) *Business plan*. [Online]. [Accessed 28 April 2015]. Available from: <http://www.entrepreneur.com/encyclopedia/business-plan>
- Filion, L.J., Ananou, C. and Schmitt, C. (2012) *Réussir sa création d'entreprise sans business plan*. Paris: Eyrolles.
- Kotler, P., Keller, K. and Manceau, D. (2012) *Marketing Management*. [14th edition]. Montreuil: Pearson.
- Lavinski, D. (2013) Business Plan Outline – 23 Point Checklist for Success. *Forbes*. [Online]. [Accessed 28 April 2015]. Available from: <http://www.forbes.com/sites/davelavinsky/2013/12/03/business-plan-outline-23-point-checklist-for-success/>
- LICP. (2015) *Tableau de bord et reporting*. [Online]. [Accessed 10 June 2015]. Available from Internet Archive: <http://web.archive.org/web/20150513051720/http://www.licp.fr/site/images/stories/pdf/BTS_cgo/p8_9_chap8.pdf>
- Université de Namur. (2013) Guide d'information. Le plan d'affaires ou business plan. *UNamur*. [Online]. [Accessed 28 April 2015]. Available from Internet Archive: <http://web.archive.org/web/20130613005419/http://www.

unamur.be/recherche/utiles/optival/formations/
OPTIVALGuidePlanAffaires.pdf>

ADDITIONAL SOURCES

- Stutely, R. (2001) *The Definitive Business Plan: The Fast-Track to Intelligent Business Planning for Executives and Entrepreneurs.* Upper Saddle River: FT Press.

50MINUTES.com
History
Business
Coaching
EL DIAGRAMA DE ISHIKAWA
Material Método Máquina
Madre Naturaleza Medida Hombres
LA GUERRA DE PALESTINA DE 1948
DOMINA EL ARTE DEL NETWORKING